Withdrawn

RUSSIA

GROLIER
EDUCATIONAL

Published for Grolier Educational
Sherman Turnpike, Danbury, Connecticut
by Marshall Cavendish Books
an imprint of Times Media Pte Ltd
Times Centre, 1 New Industrial Road, Singapore 536196
Tel: (65) 2848844 Fax: (65) 2854871
Email: te@corp.tpl.com.sg
World Wide Web:
http://www.timesone.com.sg/te

Copyright © 1997, 1999 Times Media Pte Ltd, Singapore
Fourth Grolier Printing 2000

Set ISBN: 0-7172-9099-9
Volume ISBN: 0-7172-9113-8

Library of Congress Cataloging-in-Publication Data
Russia.
p.cm. -- (Fiesta!)
Includes index.
Summary: Discusses the customs and beliefs connected to some of the special occasions celebrated in Russia, including the Festival of Winter, Women's Day, and Victory Day. Includes recipes and related activities.
ISBN 0-7172-9113-8
1. Russia (Federation) -- Social life and customs -- Juvenile literature. 2. Festivals -- Russia (Federation) -- Juvenile literature. [1. Festivals -- Russia (Federation). 2. Holidays -- Russia (Federation).
3. Russia (Federation) -- Social life and customs.]
I. Grolier Educational (Firm) II. Series: Fiesta! (Danbury, Conn.)
DK510.32.R867 1997
947--dc21
97-19378
CIP
AC

Marshall Cavendish Books Editorial Staff
Editorial Director: Ellen Dupont
Series Designer: Joyce Mason
Crafts devised and created by Susan Moxley
Music arrangements by Harry Boteler
Photographs by Bruce Mackie
Subeditors: Susan Janes, Judy Fovargue
Production: Craig Chubb

For this volume
Editor: Tessa Paul
Designer: Trevor Vertigan
Consultant: Svetlana Johnson
Editorial Assistant: Lorien Kite

Printed in Italy

Adult supervision advised for all crafts and recipes particularly those involving sharp instruments and heat.

CONTENTS

RUSSIA:

Russia was a Communist state for 80 years. In 1992 the political system changed. The country is now a democracy.

▶ **Moscow** is the capital of Russia. St. Basil's Cathedral lies within the Kremlin, which also contains palaces and Russia's modern political buildings.

◀ **Icons** are found in Russian churches. Not all icons are as richly decorated as this. Many are simply painted on wood. Most Christians in Russia are members of the Russian Orthodox Church, a very old branch of the Christian Church.

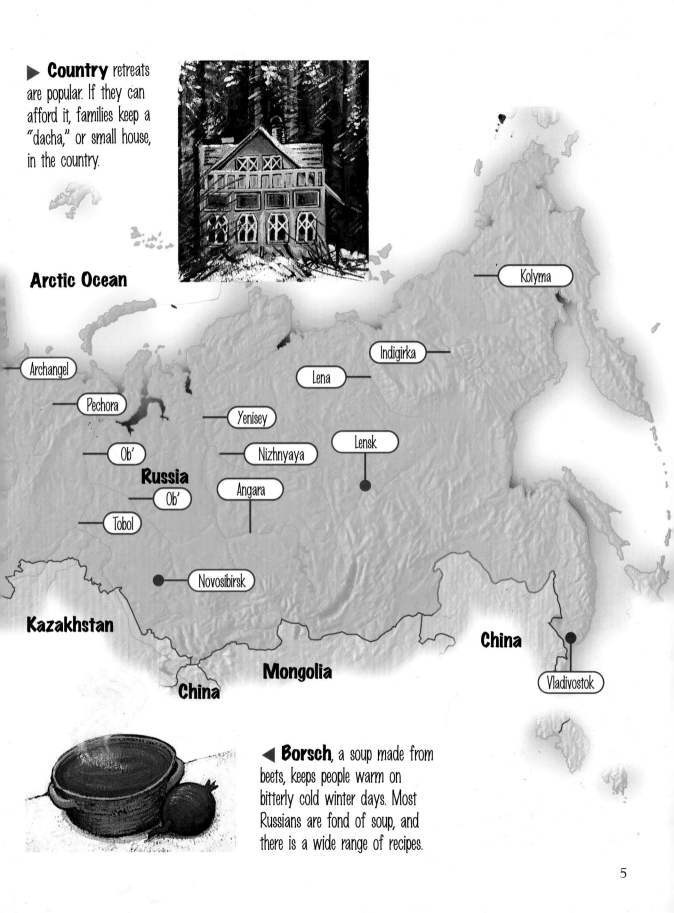

► **Country** retreats are popular. If they can afford it, families keep a "dacha," or small house, in the country.

Arctic Ocean

Kolyma

Indigirka

Archangel

Lena

Pechora

Yenisey

Lensk

Ob'

Nizhnyaya

Russia

Ob'

Angara

Tobol

Novosibirsk

Kazakhstan

China

Mongolia

China

Vladivostok

◄ **Borsch**, a soup made from beets, keeps people warm on bitterly cold winter days. Most Russians are fond of soup, and there is a wide range of recipes.

RELIGIONS

For centuries the people of Russia were Christians, but the leaders of the Russian Revolution tried to change their faith.

The Romanov family ruled Russia for three hundred years. They were not called kings and queens but were known as *tsars* and *tsarinas*. In 1917 the people rose against the tsar, and the leaders of the Revolution also rebelled against the church.

They thought the priests were too close to the tsar and his government. After they murdered the tsar and his family, these leaders shut down most of the churches and made life very difficult for the priests. The revolutionaries took away land and money belonging to the church.

However, the church in Russia had a long history and was loved by many, who prayed for its return. In 1981 a more liberal Communist government allowed some churches to open. Once more Christians could celebrate their faith. The Communists lost power in 1991. All churches are now

The Russian Orthodox Church developed from the early Christian empire of Byzantium. Priests' ornate robes use designs from this old empire.

open and many people attend services.

The church in Russia is not a branch of the Catholic or Protestant churches. It has its roots in early Christian religion in the East. In Christianity's earliest days an important center of Christianity was the city of Byzantium, now Istanbul in Turkey. The Russian Orthodox Church is a branch of this old form of Christianity.

The Russian church follows ancient rituals and encourages a mystic, unquestioning belief. It is famous for its "holy men." They are called *startsy* in Russian. When the tsars ruled, startsy roamed the country preaching God's words. They had no belongings. The people fed them and gave them shelter. Orthodox priests are allowed to marry and have families but some choose to be monks, holy men who never marry.

Today the young do not know about Christianity. Older people were taught the faith as children. No one knows what will happen when they are gone.

GREETINGS FROM **RUSSIA!**

When Russia was ruled by Communists, it was the center of the Union of Soviet Socialist Republics. The USSR was the biggest country in the world. It stretched from the edge of Europe across Asia to the borders of China. It controlled many nationalities who spoke many languages. In 1991 the USSR fell apart.

Russia is now a smaller country and controls few other states. The official language is Russian. It uses the Cyrillic alphabet. This was used throughout the old empire, so many Asian languages are also written in Cyrillic.

How do you say...

Hello

Ztravstveechye

Goodbye

Do-svidanya

Thank you

Spasseeba

Peace

Meer

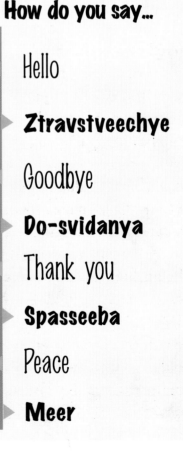

CHRISTMAS

For over seventy years Christmas was not officially celebrated in the Russian church. Now the joyous service for the birth of Christ is again part of Russian life.

Christmas in the Russian Orthodox Church is celebrated on another day from the day used by Roman Catholic and Protestant churches. This is because the Orthodox Church uses a different religious calendar. Its Christmas falls in January.

Churches are open all night on Christmas Eve. Worshipers stay as long as they can; some may stay right through the night. Everybody lights a candle, believing that the flames show the spirit of Jesus Christ is alive in the world. On this occasion the

Icons are religious paintings. Usually made of wood they are found in every church. Icons are also carried on journeys or kept at home. Stained glass light adds to the beauty of icons.

priests wear special robes embroidered in gold and red.

Ritual is important. The Russian Orthodox prayers follow exactly the same pattern of words and actions at every service.

On Christmas Eve the Eucharist service, also called the liturgy, is solemn but joyous. For hundreds of years the music and words

The churches were designed to be majestic and mysterious. The dim glow of candles fills the buildings. The sweet smell of incense comess from fine brass censerss.

of the liturgy have not altered. As morning breaks, priests prepare for the Holy Eucharist This is a ritual focused on bread and wine. It is done in memory of Christ and starts the day on His birthday.

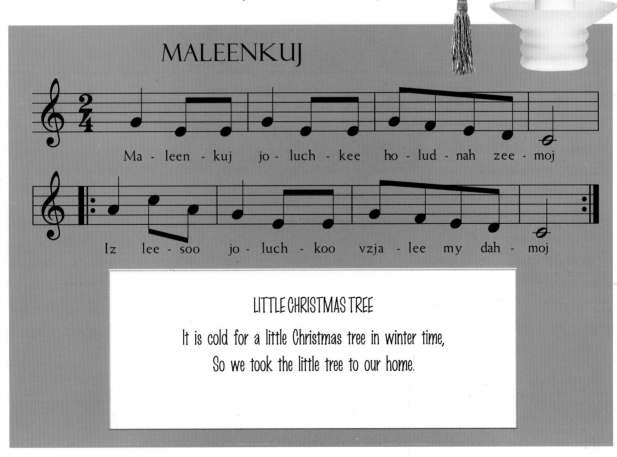

MALEENKUJ

Ma - leen - kuj jo - luch - kee ho - lud - nah zee - moj

Iz lee - soo jo - luch - koo vzja - lee my dah - moj

LITTLE CHRISTMAS TREE

It is cold for a little Christmas tree in winter time,
So we took the little tree to our home.

FESTIVAL OF WINTER

The Festival of Winter begins just before Christmas and ends in March with bonfires and ashes. It is a time for giving presents and going to parties, the theater, and the ballet. It is a time for skating and tobogganing.

In Russia winter has a special quality. The crisp, cold weather lasts for such a long time the Russians have learned to enjoy their climate.

They have a Festival of Winter when the parks are open through the long evenings, and everyone is outdoors. Christmas was not recognized in the USSR, but Christmas trees have always been put up in parks and the foyers of the theaters at this season.

Most Russian towns have enormous and splendid parks. In the summer they are used as places for sports, but in winter they are magically lighted up and transformed with decorated trees.

Family groups in their fur coats walk

These figures represent Cossack dancers who come from southern Russia. They are famous for their powerful dancing style of strong, high kicks. Folk music is played on a balalaika, a triangular type of guitar, and may be accompanied by flutes. Choral singing plays an important role in folk music.

about taking the air. Huge *samovars* steam at tea stalls, and *blinis,* a type of small pancake, are for sale at every corner. The children t o b o g g a n while adults go roaming t h r o u g h the forests on cross country s k i s .

People iceskate over the frozen paths and rivers. Dance groups in traditional folk clothes entertain the crowds. Folk musicians perform in the parks.

The theaters and ballet companies are very busy at this time. Children, especially, are treated with visits to the ballet, opera, concerts, and theater. Factories will organize outings for children of employees. If a child has a birthday in winter, a lovely fairy tale girl, the Snow Maiden, is asked to visit and bring gifts in her horse-drawn *troika*.

Even the bears in this hand carved toy are enjoying their samovar as every good Russian does.

Religious tradition marks January 19 as the baptism of Christ. The baptism ritual involves water. There is an old belief that on January 19, if a girl gazes into the water blessed by a priest, she will see the image of her future husband.

Also on this day some Russians dive through holes in the ice to take a swim in the freezing waters of one of Russia's many rivers. They emerge to jog across the ice. These brave people are known as the *morzhy* – the walruses.

11

BLINIS

MAKES 30

1¼ cups milk
1½ tsp active-dry yeast
2 tsp sugar
⅓ cup all-purpose flour
⅓ cup buckwheat flour
¼ tsp salt
2 large eggs, separated
1 tbsp butter, melted, plus extra for cooking

1 Heat ¼ cup milk until tepid. Pour into a bowl. Stir in yeast and sugar. Let stand until foamy.

2 Sift both flours and salt into a large bowl. Heat ½ cup of milk until tepid. Add this and the yeast liquid to the flour. Cover and let stand in warm place 2½ hours.

3 Warm remaining milk until tepid. Beat in egg yolks and butter. Beat into batter. Re-cover and let stand 30 minutes.

4 Beat egg whites until stiff peaks form. Fold into batter.

5 Lightly butter skillet over medium heat. Add 1 tbsp batter at a time and cook 3 minutes. Flip over and cook on other side. Continue until all batter is used.

Russians eat blini with sour cream and caviar or, as in this picture, with salmon. You might like them better with jelly!

Some inhabitants of the northern parts of Russia carve ice houses, and Russian tourists may take a trip to show their children this glittering, magical sight.

In the Christian tradition the end of winter is marked by a carnival, followed by Lent. During the many years when the churches were closed, Lent and Easter were mostly forgotten by the Russian people. However, they kept some rituals to mark

The colors used in folk art echo the tones of church icons, the only art most people knew in tsarist Russia.

the turning of winter into spring. They ate *blinis* because their circular shape is symbolic of the sun.

There is one ritual followed by the farmers of Russia that goes back centuries before Christianity. This was a time when it was believed that the changing seasons were caused by magic forces and invisible spirits.

This ancient celebration to end winter is known as *Maslenitsa,* and it occurs on the second Sunday of March. In the country farmers and their families make straw figures of *Bajarynya,* a grand but gentle lady. Bonfires are built, and these fires light up the evenings. Then the straw Bajarynyas are burned, and their ashes are scattered across the fields. This used to be a way of

A samovar, patterned with folk art, brightens the Russian winter. It is flanked by a tin of Russian tea, a favorite drink as people wander the parks during the Festival of Winter.

asking the spirits to give the farmers a good spring and a rich harvest in the coming year.

No matter what system governs the nation, old beliefs live on. Even under the rule of Communism, when such practices were frowned upon, farmers made their bonfires as they had for centuries before Christians, tsars or Communists.

THE FROST, THE SUN, AND THE WIND

Many people in Russia live in the country and are farmers.

They watch the weather carefully so that the crops grow,

and the animals are herded indoors when it is cold or wet.

This is a folk story about understanding the weather.

ONE DAY THE FROST, the Sun, and the Wind were walking on a road in the countryside, when they came across a kind peasant.

"Greetings," said the farmer as he walked by. The Frost, the Sun, and the Wind continued walking. The Frost thought about the friendly farmer.

"Which one of us was that polite farmer greeting?" he asked.

"He was talking to me so that I would not burn him with my heat," the Sun answered immediately.

"He was talking to me," said the Frost, "so I would not freeze him with my cold and chilling embrace."

"You are both wrong," said the Wind. "The kind peasant was talking to me."

The three of them continued to argue about the matter. Finally they agreed to find the farmer and ask him to give them the answer. They found him further down the road.

"Whom were you greeting when we met you earlier?" they asked.

The farmer told them that he was talking only to the Wind. Both the Sun and the Frost were outraged by the farmer's response.

"I am going to burn you to a crisp with my hot rays," threatened the Sun. But the Wind whistled in the farmer's ears, "Don't worry, I will cool you off with my breeze."

"Well, I'm going to freeze you until you're covered in ice," bellowed the Frost. "Don't worry, farmer," said the Wind, "If I don't blow, there can be no Frost."

The farmer knew he had been wise in understanding the weather.

NEW YEAR

"Novy God" is the Russian for New Year. It is the children's favorite holiday because this is the time for presents and candy.

New Year is the biggest holiday in Russia. On the night of December 31 every child is very excited and hardly sleeps at all. They are all waiting for Grandfather Frost, who is called *Ded-Moroz* in Russian. He comes with his helper, the Snow Maiden, called *Snegurochka*, to give out presents.

These two travel in a *troika*, a sled that is drawn by three horses. Each year in all the towns and tiny villages a girl is chosen to be the Snow Maiden. She is always blonde and dressed in white and blue with sparkling jewels. Not only does she appear on New Year's Day, but she visits parks and parties all through the Festival of Winter.

Before the children are given presents,

Russian folk dishes decorated with themes of wild flowers and strawberries are popular tableware.

A samovar is a Russian kettle. A teapot is fitted on the top so it is heated by the steam. There is a strong brew in the teapot. A little of the brew is poured into a cup, then diluted with hot kettle water.

they sing or recite a story to Grandfather Frost and his helper.

On New Year's Eve families traditionally gather together. In every home there is a little Christmas tree, with chocolates, bags of candy, tangerines, and apples for the children. Family and friends exchange greeting cards.

Russian families will bring out their most colorful tableware for the festive season.

A festive meal is prepared. It includes *borsch*, a red beet soup, and beef stroganoff, a type of stew, pickled tomatoes, and salads.

At midnight the New Year is celebrated with champagne. It is also drunk with the meal, as are many cups of tea.

PINK POTATO SALAD

SERVES 4 TO 6
4 cooked beets, cooled
4 boiled potatoes, cooled
2 cups cooked diced carrots, cooled
4 scallions
2 dill pickles
1 can (14 ounces) peas
Salt and pepper
2 tbsp chopped fresh parsley
2 tbsp chopped fresh dill
½ cup Italian salad dressing

1 Ask an adult to peel and cut beets into small cubes. Put in large salad bowl. Ask adult to peel and cube potatoes. Add to bowl.
2 Thinly slice scallions and dill pickles. Add to salad bowl.
3 Drain peas, and add to bowl.
4 Using a spoon, mix all ingredients together. Juices from beets will turn salad pink.
5 Add salt and pepper. Sprinkle with parsley and dill. Cover with plastic wrap and chill.
6 Remove salad from refrigerator about 15 minutes before serving. Toss with Italian dressing to serve.

Traditional Russian potato salad is a colorful mix of cooked vegetables and fresh herbs. It is a favorite dish at New Year.

THE SNOW MAIDEN

The opera "The Snow Maiden" by the Russian composer Rimsky-Korsakov was inspired by this story. He liked to base his operas on Russian folk tales, like that of Snegurochka the Snow Maiden. Operas often end tragically, and Rimsky-Korsakov's version of the story is even sadder than the legend we tell here.

LONG AGO there lived a girl called Snegurochka. She was the daughter of the Fairy Spring and the winter-god, King Frost. Every year the Fairy Spring and King Frost ran from the summer and hid in the icy wastes of northern Siberia. There they would also hide their daughter, Snegurochka – for if Sun were ever to see her, she would die.

When Snegurochka turned sixteen, her parents realized that she had to go out into the world. Before leaving for Siberia, Spring gave her daughter a word of advice. "Be sure never to fall in love," she said. "As long as there is no love in your heart, you are invisible to Sun, and he cannot hurt you."

Snegurochka was a kind, beautiful girl. Wherever she went, she was liked, and she lived a carefree life. One day a young prince named Misgir saw Snegurochka and fell deeply in love with her. Misgir tried to win her hand, but, remembering her mother's advice, Snegurochka took no notice of him.

The tsar heard of Misgir's sadness. He called Misgir and Snegurochka to his court. The tsar asked her who her lover was. She replied that she had no lover. "What!" boomed the tsar. "I will offer a reward to anyone who can win the love of Snegurochka."

Later that day there was a huge party. Many loving young couples were

arm-in-arm. Snegurochka felt sad. "If only I could fall in love," she sighed.

Snegurochka ran away from the feast and called out to her mother. "Let me fall in love," she cried. When Fairy Spring saw the tears on her daughter's face, she gave her daughter her blessing.

When Snegurochka went back to the party, Misgir came straight over and asked for her hand in marriage. She happily accepted. But the next day, as Snegurochka and Misgir stood waiting for the tsar to marry them, tragedy struck. Sun saw the warmth in her heart, and Snegurochka the little Snow Maiden melted away.

The Snow Maiden can only come to the world when it is cold. But Sun could not melt her kindness, and each year she brings gifts to all the children.

WOMEN'S DAY

International Women's Day was declared an annual event in 1914. This day celebrates the equality and dignity of women.

In the Danish city of Copenhagen in 1910 a group of women came together for a very important meeting. They wanted to improve the lives of women all over the world. At this time most women were treated unfairly by the laws of their countries, and very few were able to earn their own living.

Most women were cared for by their fathers, brothers, and husbands. They had very little freedom to travel or study without the permission of the men guarding their lives. The group

Some husbands give their wives food blenders or toasters on this day, but most look for less useful, fun things as gifts. Jewelry and perfumes are popular, but Russians love to give and receive flowers.

who gathered in 1910 decided that women should try to change the system controlling their life and work. They said everyone ought to be reminded

Women's Day cards are on sale everywhere, and every woman hopes to get one on March 8.

of the status of women. Every year there should be one day dedicated to women.

International Women's Day is on March 8. Most countries recognize this day, but few celebrate it as a festival day.

However, in the USSR and now, in modern Russia, this is a special day. Women are given presents and treats by their husbands and sons. In factories and offices the male workers give gifts to all the women with whom they work.

Children will bring flowers to their female teachers and make cards for them. They also give their mothers and aunts similar gifts. It is also a time when all children try to help their mothers and do favors around the house. Perfume, jewelry, and fur coats are the sort of presents men give to women close to them.

Candies and chocolates are treats suitable for festive occasions. Packed in decorative boxes, they have become familiar gifts on Women's Day.

In 1914, for the first time, women in the United States, Germany, Switzerland, Austria, and Russia celebrated Women's Day. These other countries still mark the day, but only the USSR, as Russia became after the Revolution in 1917, made March 8 a national holiday.

During the early years of the celebration the day tended to be very political. At meetings and conferences women met to discuss their rights in the workplace. A lot of time was given to changing the laws in Russia and elsewhere.

Women did not want to be treated as inferior to men and in need of guidance. In most of the countries of the western world these issues are no longer a problem. Women do now have status closer to men's.

However, Russian women continue to enjoy special treatment on International Women's Day. Those who have achieved great success in their work or as mothers are given medals and honors by the state. And in homes, schools and workplaces across the land all ordinary Russian women are also given respect and honor on this day.

MAKE A BOWL

Russian folk art shows a love of red flowers, such as poppies, and red fruit, strawberries in particular. This bowl can be filled with candy or cookies, and it will be a perfect gift for your mother.

YOU WILL NEED
Balloon • Newspaper
Wallpaper paste
Cardboard • Masking tape
Poster paints
Clear varnish

1 Blow up a balloon. Cover the balloon with strips of paper covered with wallpaper paste. Make an even, smooth surface. Leave to dry. When it is dry, draw a line around the middle of the balloon shape, then cut the shape in half, following the line. You will now have two bowl shapes.

2 Take a strip of cardboard to use as the base of your bowl. Trim it to suit the size of your bowl then fold the strip into a circle and stick ends together with masking tape. Attach it to the base of one bowl with masking tape. Cover the bowl inside and out with a base of black paint. Paint the red and gold designs over this. Coat with clear varnish.

We have chosen a traditional Russian design, but of course, you can choose your own colors and designs. Create a bowl to suit

VICTORY DAY

Every year the soldiers who fought against Germany in the Great Patriotic War are honored on Victory Day, May 9. It was on this day in 1945 that the war ended.

The Russians will not easily forget World War II (1939–1945). They call this war the Great Patriotic War. Over 20 million Russians died in the fighting during the German invasion of "Mother Russia." When the Red Army defeated the German Army in a battle at the city of Stalingrad in 1943, the Germans never recovered, and the world war in Europe ended in 1945.

The Great Patriotic War was a bitter conflict. The old people, women, and chidren, who did not go to the war front, also suffered. The invading Germans killed many. The fighting stopped vital deliveries of food and fuel, so many families starved and froze to death. Every Russian family was hurt by the war. This is why Victory Day is so important.

The Grave of the Unknown Soldier is in a Moscow park. The

The art of Soviet Russia aimed to show the best qualities of the ordinary people. This statue expresses the belief in the calm courage of the men of the Red Army. Military badges are treasured and displayed on Victory Day.

grave is marked by the Eternal Flame and stands close by the Kremlin, which was once a tsarist palace and is now a state building. The Russian President and many other dignitaries lay wreaths.

Veterans, who are men who fought for their country, meet up with their old regimental group. They gather in front of the Bolshoi Theater. They wear parts of their old war uniforms. Black coats, fur hats, red blouses, and epaulets bring color to the streets on Victory Day.

Most are carrying wreaths and bunches of flowers as they slowly walk towards the gigantic Grave of the Unknown Soldier. Many display medals earned in the war.

In all the towns and villages across Russia other veterans are gathering at their

Banners celebrate the Red Army. The army of the USSR was called the Red Army because the color symbolized Communism.

assembly points, such as the town hall or a farm office. They, too, are dressed to show they are old soldiers.

The veterans form processions down the streets. They lay their wreaths and flowers at the war memorial in their town, or at the graves of their relatives

25

and friends who died in the Patriotic War. The veterans march together, but they are joined by their children and grandchildren so that this sad anniversary is remembered by all Russians.

Local leaders like the mayor and police chief imitate the President in Moscow, when they lay wreaths on local memorials.

Shortly before the USSR collapsed, the Soviet army was at war in Afghanistan.

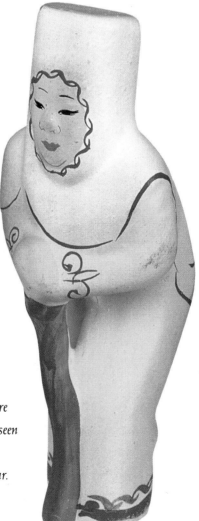

Before the war peasants such as these were found near the Polish border. They had seen the tsar fall and lived with Communism. They helped win the Great Patriotic War.

This is a country on the old southern borders of the USSR. On Victory Day, the 25,000 soldiers who died in the Afghan War are honored too and these veterans also gather in their former regiments. These men are much younger than the old veterans of the Great Patriotic War. Their celebrations are noisier than those of their grandfathers!

When night falls on Victory Day, Red Square, which is right in the the center of Moscow, becomes flooded with light. Huge crowds gather there to watch a fine display of fireworks.

ANTHEM OF THE SOVIET UNION

Sah - jus nee - roo shee - myj rees - poob - lik svah - bod nyh splah -

tee - lah i ve - kee mah - goo - chi - ja Roos Dah

zdrahv - stvoo - it so - zdahn - nyj vo - lij ri ro - dahv ji -

dee - nyj mah - goo - chij Sah - vet - skij Sah - jus

The indestructable union of free republics Was cemented forever by Great Russia. Long live the Soviet Union, united and mighty, Created by the will of the people.

A keyring with an image of the old tsarist buildings and the revolutionary Peoples' Palace makes a fine gift on Victory Day, as does a box of cakes with a lucky horseshoe cover.

of soldiers, who were usually male. So the day has become one when fathers, brothers, and sons, are made to feel special. Fathers are given little gifts such as after-shave lotion or colognes. Candy and flowers are also popular presents.

But Victory Day remains a day when Russians express their patriotism, a day to celebrate the national pride in the fight for their land.

Similar festivities occur on this evening all over the country with fireworks, bands, and street gatherings.

Victory Day is a day about the bravery

EASTER

This festival is slowly becoming part of life again. In the days before Communism it was a time to fast and mourn, and the faithful spent long hours in prayer.

A jeweled Easter egg is stored in a carved wooden case, lined with silver. Holy images such as that of Jesus were popular on eggs.

I n the days of the tsar the church was closely tied to the lives of almost every Russian. Priests were found in every village, and holy men were familiar sights in the country.

Russians celebrated the Orthodox Easter with deep respect. In the forty days of Lent before Easter believers fasted and did not eat meat. Icons were draped with embroidered sheets. Services to mourn the death of Christ were very long. Priests believed they should keep vigil and suffer for the same number of hours that

These wooden eggs are typical of gifts exchanged by country folk on Easter Sunday.

Jesus Christ hung dying on the cross.

Easter Sunday was joyous, celebrating the belief that Christ rose from the dead. Eggs were given as gifts. Country people often painted boiled eggs or carved eggs from wood. They decorated the eggs with images copied from icon paintings. During the reign of the three tsars a family of jewelers, the Fabergés, made eggs of precious gems set in silver and gold, for rich people. These eggs also bore holy images.

MAKE A STURGEON

When the tsar and rich landowners were in power, they ate sturgeon at Easter. The fish, which is large, was poached in wine. Another rare delicacy is *caviar*, the eggs of the sturgeon. Even today, this dish is extremely expensive. Make a model of this beautiful sturgeon. Give it glorious colors and patterns, as befits this fine, rare fish.

YOU WILL NEED
2 cups of flour
2 tbl vegetable oil • 2 cups
salt • Water • Poster paints

1 To make the dough, mix the flour, salt, and oil. Add water to make a thick paste.. Mix and knead well with hands. Roll out the dough on a floured surface. Cut out the shape you require — fish or eagle (or both!). Pattern the dough with a fork or toothpick. Place on a baking tray and bake in a cool oven for 2 to 3 hours until the figures are hard to the touch. Use poster paints to decorate the creatures.

The tsar had an eagle as his symbol of state. You may choose to mold this three-headed heraldic eagle.

29

REVOLUTION DAY

The 1917 Revolution promised to give power to the people. October 27 is a day of hope and celebrates great changes in the political life of "Mother Russia."

The last tsar of Russia, Nicholas II, was known as "Bloody Nicholas" because in 1905 his soldiers shot many hundreds of people demonstrating for a better life.

On October 27, 1917 the people rose in anger and stormed the Winter Palace in St. Petersburg. The Russian Revolution had begun.

Leaders promised that every Russian would have a better life under a socialist system. The state owned all farms and factories. There were

СЛАВА ВЕЛИКОМУ ОКТЯБРЮ !

jobs and homes for everybody. But no one was free. In 1991 the Russians changed the socialist system for democracy.

Revolution Day used to involve street parades of the Red Army, weapons, and tanks. Leaders gave

Lenin was the great revolutionary leader who toppled the tsar. His body has been preserved and now lies in state in the Kremlin..

speeches about the benefits of socialism. Since 1991 the day is less solemn. It has a holiday feel of parties, good food, and fun.

WORDS TO KNOW

Censer: A container that is used for burning incense during a religious service.

Communism: A method of running a country in which property is owned by the government. Under Communism people work at the job they are best able to do and are paid according to their needs.

Cossacks: A people of Southern Russia and the Ukraine known for their great horsemanship.

Eastern Orthodox Church: One of the main branches of Christianity. It consists of a group of national churches, found mainly in eastern Europe and the Middle East.

Epaulet: A decorative shoulder strap on a military uniform.

Incense: A mixture of gum and spice that gives off a pleasing smell when burned. Incense is often used in religious services.

Liberal: Open to new ideas, not strict.

Mystic: Having to do with mysterious forces which people are unable to understand.

Patriotic: Proud of one's country.

Political: Having to do with the running of a country and its government.

Revolutionaries: People who believe in putting an end to the current government by force, and replacing it with another type of government.

Ritual: A religious ceremony which must be performed in a certain way or order.

Russian Orthodox Church: The Christian church in Russia, that is neither Catholic nor Protestant, but part of the Eastern Orthodox Church.

Russian Revolution: The violent removal of the Tsar in 1917, which was followed by the setting up of a Communist government.

Tsar: The word for king in Russian.

ACKNOWLEDGMENTS

WITH THANKS TO:

Articles of Faith, Religious Articles and Resources for Education, Bury icon, lamp p8-9. Hobgoblin Music, Crawley balalaika p11. Iconastas Russian Fine Art, London statue of soldiers p24-25. Svetlana Johnson all Russian eggs, bowls, spoons, jewelry, and toys. Vale Antiques, London Cossack dancers p10-11, samovar p16-17.

PHOTOGRAPHS BY:

All photographs by Bruce Mackie except: John Elliott p17(bottom). Cover photograph by Trip/A Lyaskov.

ILLUSTRATIONS BY:

Alison Fleming p4-5. Mountain High Maps ® Copyright © 1993 Digitial Wisdom, Inc. p4-5. Tracy Rich p7. John Spencer p15. Alison Fleming p19.

SET CONTENTS